THE PRACTICAL GUIDE TO BECOMING LOVE

How to Practice Love Every Day
(so you can stop suffering, feel joyful
and help humanity live in peace)

THE ORIGINAL EDITION

Alexander De Jordy

it came from Love

The information in this book is meant to supplement, not replace, proper BECOME LOVE training. Like any training involving patience, forgiveness, gratitude and compassion, becoming Love poses some inherent risk. The writer has made every effort to supply the reader with accurate and practical information on how to BECOME LOVE, but advises readers to take full responsibility for their safety and know their limits. Do not take risks beyond your level of experience, aptitude, training, and comfort level.

WHAT DOES IT MEAN TO "BECOME LOVE"?

All of your actions are infinitely, immediately and unconditionally patient, forgiving, grateful and compassionate towards yourself and others.

Everything you do is Loving.

This is the goal.

THE STEPS TO BECOME LOVE

STEP 1: SIT-DOWN MEDITATION

STEP 2: STAND-UP MEDITATION

STEP 3: FULL-TIME MEDITATION

INTRODUCTION

You can practice Love just like anything else you'd want to get better at. If you wanted to blend concealer makeup better, you'd practice blending concealer. If you wanted a better serve in tennis, you'd practice hitting serves. And if you wanted to become the most Loving version of yourself, you'd practice patience, forgiveness, gratitude and compassion.

That's exactly what this guide shows you how to do. And I mean *exactly*. I'm not going tell you what you *should* do and share nice anecdotes from people that have done it. There are a million self-help books like that. I'm going to tell you exactly *how*. As in, you need to do <u>this</u> at <u>this</u> time, then <u>this</u> at <u>this</u> time, and here's exactly how to do <u>this</u>. All you have do is follow my instructions and practicing Love will still be the hardest thing you've ever attempted.

Sorry.

Look, you *can* practice Love, but it's really hard. I won't hide it. It's way harder than losing belly fat or becoming a millionaire. In order to practice Love you're going to have to learn to control your thoughts and actions. Not drown out your thoughts. Not rationalize your actions. Be in control of them. Learning to be in control of your thoughts and actions is called *taming your mind* and it's the hardest thing a human being can learn to do.

So... why would you want to do it?

Because <u>not</u> being in control of your thoughts and actions is why you suffer.

Without getting too deep into it right now, we all run on this automatic and unconscious behaviour I call 'old code'. Old code causes us to be impatient, resentful, ungrateful and judgemental. These unconscious responses make you feel bad. When you can learn to stop responding in these ways, and instead respond in Loving ways, you will stop suffering and feel joyful. It's actually quite simple. It just requires a lot of practice.

So, just like getting better at applying makeup, or playing tennis, you can get better at being a Loving person by practicing patience, forgiveness, gratitude and compassion—what I call *The 4 Practicable Actions of Love*. By putting Love into a practicable action ("practicing Love") you will learn to override the old code that causes you suffering. You will learn to make Love your 'new code', and eventually, with enough practice, you can even *become* Love. As in, all of your actions are Loving; everything you do is Loving. Which isn't woo-woo at all. It's just you-you, at your most Loving, living life, feeling joyful.

Let's be clear though, joy is not euphoria. I'm not promising you'll feel like you've had 17 cups of coffee all the time. Joy is a deep, deep peace that feels *good*. Which is really what everyone wants. We spend a lot of money trying to buy temporary peace—shopping, drinking, entertaining. Practicing Love leads to lasting peace. That's a pretty good reason to practice.

So it really comes down to how badly you want to stop suffering and feel joyful. Bad enough to do something really hard? Here's some extra incentive: You becoming Love is the only way humanity will ever live in peace.

We need more Loving people. Right now. Because the more people on the planet consciously choosing Love over old code, the more peaceful the planet becomes. When you practice Love you will influence your circle of friends, which will influence your community, and your country, until eventually, with enough people practicing Love, humanity lives in peace. Finally. That chain reaction of Love starts with you and me.

You BECOME LOVE by practicing Love. That's what this guide sets out to show, and exactly how to do it. This guide is short and written in modern practical language. It fits any belief system, any affiliation, any background. Everyone can practice Love.

Last thoughts before we begin: The guide is repetitive. It has to be. There really isn't that much to learn, but what there is requires repetition to cement. Also, you might be offended by some of what you read. It may feel like I'm attacking you for not having control of your thoughts and actions. This is a very natural response. Our minds don't like being told what to do—not by us, definitely not by other people. So please remember this:

I struggle too. I've struggled with old code my entire life and I continue struggling to this day—although a *lot* less than before. I know the pain of wanting to be at peace and not knowing how to get there. That's why I wrote this guide. I wrote it for me so I can share it with you. Because—and I say this without a hint of BS—I Love you. And yet, I've never met you. How is that possible?

Because I practice Love every day.

Let me show you how.

Alexander De Jordy
Toronto
February, 2024

compassion patience forgiveness gratitude
BECOME
LOVE

STEP 1: SIT-DOWN MEDITATION

WHY BECOME LOVE?

To BECOME LOVE is a life goal. It's a better goal for your life.

Think about the current goal of modern life. It's whatever the ego wants: success, status, influence, entertainment, attention, acquisition, pleasure. The problem is, no matter how much you get, your ego will never be satisfied, making you impatient, resentful, ungrateful, judgemental.

If the goal of your life is to satisfy your ego, then every challenge in your life is an obstacle preventing you from being happy.

But when you make the goal of your life to BECOME LOVE, all of the challenges in your life are opportunities to practice your goal. You can be excited for every little thing that happens.

Stop trying to satisfy your ego. Use your life to BECOME LOVE instead. It's a better goal.

You achieve the goal with meditation. Stop. You don't have to sigh or roll your eyes. Chances are you don't even know what meditation is.

So forget what you think you know about meditation and start over.

WHAT IS MEDITATION?

Meditation is practice.

What are you practicing?

Taming your mind.

Meditation is the practice of taming your mind.

What is taming your mind?

Learning to be in control of your thoughts and actions.

WHY TAME YOUR MIND?

Because you can't BECOME LOVE until you tame your mind.

Imagine your mind is a computer. Your mind/ computer runs on 'old code'. Code tells computers what to do. Our old code tells us what to do.

Old code is our unconscious thoughts and actions, it's our automatic responses we picked up after getting emotionally hurt and we continue to act out these responses unknowingly whether we want to or not.

For example: You like a person but they like someone else, so you feel jealous of that someone else, you resent the person you like, you get angry with yourself, and you overeat. Unconsciously expressing jealousy, resentment, anger, and compulsive behaviour—that's old code. Or, you have a job interview and you're so nervous that you can barely speak. Uncontrollable anxiety, that's old code. And the source of all violence is old code, too. Old code causes us suffering.

This is how old code works: First, our ego gets hurt and in response we feel an emotion like anger, envy or fear. Then, we *express* that emotion automatically through unconscious thoughts and actions. We become impatient, resentful, ungrateful, judgemental. Old code is the automatic and unconscious *expression* of emotion.

If you could decide that even though your mind is angry, envious or fearful there's no reason to *express* anger, envy or fear, and instead choose to express patience, forgiveness, gratitude and compassion—you'd always be at peace. You can do that if you tame your mind. Taming your mind ends suffering.

Your specific old code responses are influenced by your DNA, parents, friends, culture, media, emotional pain and trauma. But ultimately, your old code is written and sustained by your ego.

Until you tame your mind, your ego controls your mind.

And your ego loves old code.

WHAT IS EGO?

In the computer analogy, ego is an out-of-control program that runs the old code that controls your computer/mind.

In reality, **ego is a desire to be separate**. This can be a tough concept to understand.

There is no area of your brain labelled 'ego'. You won't find ego on an MRI. Ego is a *desire* of your mind to be separate from other people. Why? Because a very long time ago the desire to be separate from predators kept humans alive. Over time this desire to be separate evolved from a survival instinct into a selfish instinct. Now your ego wants to be separate so you can get what other people have, or maybe get even more than they have. **Ego is separateness**, or in other words, out-of-control selfishness. But the cost of wanting to be separate so you can get more and more and more for yourself is suffering.

The reward for wanting everyone, including yourself, to have what they need, is feeling joyful. So how do you do this? How do you feel joyful instead of suffering?

You change the goal of your life. **You BECOME LOVE instead of trying to satisfy your ego**. You choose Oneness over separateness.

The opposite of separateness is Oneness, which is another word for Love. Love is Oneness.

Oneness is our natural state. Babies are closest, they have minimal ego. But then our ego grows up, wants to be separate, chases more for itself. When our ego gets hurt chasing more and more, it writes old code to respond to the emotional pain of not getting it, because no matter what, your ego will never be satisfied. This creates a cycle: The more ego chases, the more it gets hurt, the more old code it writes, the more habitual the old code responses become. Now your ego is trapped by its own old code. It's why addicts get high. It's why people get taken advantage of over and over. It's why cultures fight each other for hundreds of years instead of trying to forgive. They're stuck in old code.

To BECOME LOVE, you must learn to override old code responses. You override old code (unconscious thoughts and actions) by replacing it with new code (conscious thoughts and actions). This is how you tame your mind.

Taming your mind means: teaching your mind new code (Love) instead of following orders from old code (ego).

Sit-down meditation is how you begin taming your mind.

WHAT IS SIT-DOWN MEDITATION?

Practice taming your mind by replacing unconscious thoughts with conscious thoughts.

When your mind wanders out of your control, you are thinking unconsciously. You know what this feels like. These are the kinds of thoughts you may try to drown out with movies, music or podcasts.

You sit-down meditate to learn to recognize these unconscious thoughts and to practice bringing your focus back to Love, over and over and over again. This is how you learn to think consciously.

Despite what you may have been told, you do not sit-down meditate to relax, and it defeats the purpose if somebody else "guides" you in meditation. Sit-down meditation is how *you* learn to stop *your* untamed mind from reverting to old code and keep it focused on Love. If somebody else tames your mind, who controls your mind?

There's nothing wrong with wanting to relax, or enjoying guided meditations, but if you want to BECOME LOVE you must learn to be in control of your own thoughts. This requires solo sit-down meditation.

So, where does the untamed mind wander to?

THE 4 DIRECTIONS OF MENTATION

Mentations are unconscious thoughts, thoughts you don't control. Thinking is thought you control, conscious thoughts. Pause and reflect honestly: How many of your thoughts throughout the day do you actually control?

It's important to note that mentations will rarely come to you as fully formed thoughts. And you won't hear them as a voice in your head. Mentations are more of an *urge* connected to a *thought fragment* that makes you *feel* a certain way. You might get the *urge* to eat pizza and have the *thought fragment*, "...pizza..." which *feels* positive. The rest of that mentation is actually, "(I want) pizza (because it will make me feel good)." You did not choose to have this thought, your mind did. That is a mentation.

These are *The 4 Directions of Mentation*, with examples:

UP: "I'm amazing."
DOWN: "I'm not amazing."
PAST: "I used to be..."
FUTURE: "I will be..."

Mentations can also come in combos:

DOWN / PAST is a worry: "I think I made a fool of myself yesterday."

FUTURE / UP is a fantasy: "When I'm a millionaire I will be happy."

Mentations are not good or bad, but they are a distraction. Practicing Love needs your full attention.

Sit-down meditation is how you learn to replace <u>un</u>conscious mentations with conscious thoughts by bringing your mind back to Love from *The 4 Directions of Mentation*.

HOW TO SIT-DOWN MEDITATE

There are many different sit-down meditation techniques. This one is designed to help you BECOME LOVE.

Sit somewhere comfortable where you won't fall asleep. The position of your legs is not important, it only matters that you stay attentive. Lotus position is good for back alignment, but it's physically difficult. Half-lotus is good. Cross-legged is good. Chair with a back, sitting with proper posture is also good.

No lying down. No headphones. No music. No incense. No alarms. Just you and your untamed mind. Everything else is unnecessary and becomes a distraction.

Breathe long breaths from your belly, in and out from your nose. Practice breathing from your belly throughout the day so it becomes natural.

Rest the tip of your tongue gently on the back of your lower teeth to avoid tongue tension. Keep your mouth slightly open to avoid jaw tension. Your hands can be in any relaxed position.

Refrain from fidgeting, itching, clearing your throat. These are <u>un</u>conscious actions that will distract you. If an itch is distracting, that's okay, practice not giving in to distractions.

Before you close your eyes, say to yourself out loud, "I am going to practice replacing unconscious mentations with conscious thoughts." You've just made your intentions clear. Stick to your intentions.

Now close your eyes and focus only on your breath. Count your breaths to 10. Your first inhale is 1, first exhale is 2. Up to 10. Then start again from 1. That's one cycle. Complete as many cycles as needed until you notice your mentations are slowing down. The more you practice, the better you will get at feeling when this happens. Aim for a minimum of two cycles and a maximum of five minutes counting breaths. You do not need to set an alarm. This sit-down technique isn't strict on timing. Timing is arbitrary and becomes a distraction. Better to focus on the number of cycles you can complete.

The reason we do this warm-up exercise is because it takes time to wrestle the mind from 'mentation mode' to 'meditation mode'. Don't force your mind to practice until you have prepared your mind. It will feel like this:

(Inhale) 1.... (Exhale) 2... Mentation: "This is boring." (DOWN)

Remember, mentations don't come as fully formed thoughts. It will come to you like an *urge* to stop meditating along with the *thought fragment*, "...boring..." which will make you *feel* uncomfortable.

Every time that happens, return your focus to your breath and keep counting. This is how we practice.

(Inhale) 3... (Exhale) 4... Mentation: "Has it been five minutes?" (PAST)

Return your focus to your breath and keep counting. Over, and over, and over again, continue this practice until your mind mentates less, or up to around five minutes.

If five minutes of counting your breaths is all you can manage for a while, that's okay. But you must keep at it every day until you can stand meditating longer than five minutes. It will require you to push past feeling uncomfortable. The more you practice, the faster you progress.

Now for the training exercise of this sit-down meditation technique. When you notice your mentations are slowing, or after five minutes, repeat to yourself slowly and silently:

Love...
Love... patience...
Love... patience... forgiveness...
Love... patience... forgiveness... gratitude...
Love... patience... forgiveness... gratitude... compassion...
Love... patience... forgiveness... gratitude... compassion... Love...
Love... patience... forgiveness... gratitude... compassion...
Love... patience... forgiveness... gratitude...
Love... patience... forgiveness...
Love... patience...
Love...
Love...
Love... patience...
(repeat)

That is one cycle.

For the multi-syllabic words, sound out each syllable (pa·tience, for·give·ness, grat·i·tude, com·pass·ion). After each word, pause slightly. In these pauses, unconscious mentations will arise. Use the next word to replace that unconscious mentation with a conscious thought. You just replaced old code with new code. This is why we practice.

As you become more comfortable with sit-down meditation, lengthen the pauses between words. Start with less than 1 second. Then 1 second. Then 2 seconds. Eventually, each cycle should take around three minutes. That's the speed. It's very slow.

Repeating five cycles of the words with a 2-second pause in-between each word will be around 15 minutes per sit-down meditation session. 15 minutes is enough. You don't need to set an alarm. It is okay if you practice 14 or 16 minutes. For a while you can check the time before starting, then check the time after finishing. Eventually, let go of the time and just practice. But always finish a cycle before choosing to end a session.

Your goal with this sit-down meditation technique is to warm-up by counting your breaths, then repeat five cycles of the words for around 15 minutes. That's it.

Constantly check to make sure you are not mindlessly repeating the words while mentating about something else. When you notice you are, return your focus to the words. Use the words to return your untamed mind from *The 4 Directions of Mentation*. **By repeating the words, you practice overriding old code with new code. This is how you BECOME LOVE.**

If you get lost, or lose track, start from the beginning of your last cycle. There is no value in scolding yourself, just restart. This practice is about getting better, not about being perfect. The goal of life is not to sit down in meditation, you sit down in meditation to practice the goal: BECOME LOVE. If it's hard, that means you need the practice.

A minimum of one sit-down session per day. Preferably two. It's like brushing your teeth. Your teeth won't rot if you brush one time. But not as clean as two.

The best time of the day to practice is a few minutes after you wake up. This starts your day consciously, influencing your behaviour for the rest of the day. Other good times to sit are right before lunch, the sleepiest time of the afternoon, and right before sleep.

Sit-down meditation will dramatically change your life. It is absolutely necessary if you want to BECOME LOVE. But it is only training.

You sit-down meditate, so that as you go through your day, you will be able to stand-up meditate.

WHAT IS STAND-UP MEDITATION?

Practice taming your mind by replacing unconscious actions with conscious actions throughout your day.

When your mind wanders to *The 4 Directions of Mentation* during sit-down meditation, these are only unconscious thoughts, mentations. When your mind wanders throughout the day, these unconscious mentations become unconscious actions. Unconscious action is how you act out old code.

Example of a mentation: "She said my makeup was too heavy last week so later I'm going to tell her her shoes are ugly." (DOWN / PAST / FUTURE / DOWN)

Instead, if you say her shoes are pretty, or even decide to say nothing at all, that is turning what could have been an unconscious action into a conscious action. The important thing is, your ego wanted to hurt her back and you chose not to. **By returning your actions to Love, you override old code unconscious actions and create new code conscious actions.**

Use *The 4 Expressions of Human Behaviour* to help you stand-up meditate.

THE 4 EXPRESSIONS OF HUMAN BEHAVIOUR

OLD CODE (EGO)

1: unconscious mentation
2: unconscious action

NEW CODE (LOVE)

3: conscious thought
4: conscious action

This is how life goes:

We try to be Love (4);
Ego mentates old code (1);
We unconsciously act out old code (2);
We remember we want to be Love (3);
We act on desire to Love (4);
Ego mentates old code (1);
We unconsciously act out old code (2);
We remember we want to be Love (3);
on and on and on;
and on and on and on...

When you can recognize throughout your day that you are thinking and acting unconsciously, and choose to think and act consciously, you are stand-up meditating.

You must practice turning unconscious mentation (1) and unconscious action (2) into conscious thought (3) and conscious action (4) in order to tame your mind and BECOME LOVE.

Example:

We tell elderly parent to take time getting dressed (4: patience);

Ego mentates, "We're going to be late for the movie." (1);

Old code unconscious response to feeling stressed is to snap at parent, "Hurry up!" (2);

We see we hurt parent. We think, "Why didn't I stay patient?" (3);

We apologize, help parent with shoehorn (4: patience, forgiveness)

You see now? This is stand-up meditating. You must do this every day as many times a day as you can. This is how you BECOME LOVE.

SIT-DOWN MEDITATION: REVIEW

It is almost impossible to control your ego's emotions/feelings. This is not the goal. We want to be in control of how we *express* these emotions. It takes a very long time to never have an unconscious mentation (1), but we *can* avoid unconscious action (2) right away. We want to use conscious thought (3) to keep our actions conscious (4).

You must first practice sit-down meditation, otherwise you won't notice <u>un</u>conscious mentations and actions in the moment. Even if you can notice them, without sit-down meditation, you won't be able to stop them. Your old code is too habitual. From the example above: You don't help your parent with the shoehorn, you don't apologize, you cancel the movie plans and storm off. Sound familiar?

Some people live their whole life stuck in unconscious mentation: never happy, always stressed, often envious. Some people live their whole life stuck in unconscious action: addicts, rageaholics, perpetual victims. These are not bad people, they are struggling with old code and need compassion. They never have the support and insight to move beyond unconscious mentation and action. You can start by helping yourself (meditation) and you can get support from others.

It is humanity's burden that not one single person is born free from ego and old code. You might think you are Love now, but what happens when you are stuck in traffic? Can't make rent? Favourite team loses? Wrong person wins? You get passed over for a promotion? You have a bad night's sleep? You get sick? Somebody offends you? Somebody dumps you? Somebody scares you?

Do you revert to old code, or do you remain Love?

Sit-down meditate so you are able to stand-up meditate.

Stand-up meditate to override old code and create new code by turning unconscious mentations and actions into conscious thoughts and actions throughout your day.

Now you are ready to practice Love.

STEP 2: STAND-UP MEDITATION

WHAT IS LOVE?

Let's be clear what Love is not.

Love is not the holiday trotted-out every mid-February; that's consumerism. Love doesn't care about shiny diamonds or fast sports cars; that's greed. Love is not the neurochemical high you feel during a relationship's honey-moon period; that's attachment. Love is not owning your partner; that's possession. Love is not even the desire to have sex; that's lust. Consumerism, greed, attachment, possession, lust are not Love; these are all ego desires in disguise.

Our ego confuses what the word 'Love' means by calling its own selfish desires 'love'. This makes Love seem shallow, irrational, conditional. What we really mean when we say, "I Love..." is, "I feel *at one* with..." Love is Oneness.

What is Oneness? Words fail. It is a feeling. Do you know, or can you imagine, the feeling a really good parent has for their child? That feeling of caring, nurturing, supportive selflessness: that's Oneness, that's Love. You know the feeling you have for a crying puppy? That feeling that you would do anything to help: that's Oneness, that's Love. Oneness is feeling —truly feeling—that e v e r y o n e is your family regardless of how different or messed up they are: that's Love.

The feeling of Oneness, the feeling of Love, is joy.

We would feel joy all day were it not for our unconscious mentations and actions, our old code. The old code that makes us feel angry, envious, fearful; the old code that makes us act impatient, resentful, ungrateful, judgemental, selfish—that is what blocks us from feeling Oneness, feeling Love, feeling joyful.

As you start to practice Love every day you will learn to stop joy-blocking old code. You will create the new code that allows you to feel at one with other people.

You will feel the benefits of practicing Love immediately. Love is not a light switch, it's not on or off; Love increases incrementally.

This is repetitive but it needs to be repeated: **The only way to stop suffering and feel joyful is to tame your mind and BECOME LOVE**. And the only way to BECOME LOVE is to override your old code sustained by your ego.

OVERRIDE OLD CODE / EGO

Are you able to see now that the majority of your suffering is caused by ego and old code unconscious behaviour? Automatically expressing anger, resentment, envy, entitlement, arrogance, complacency, panic, fear—these are all old code responses to when your ego doesn't get what it wants.

Are you able to see now that the vast majority of suffering on this planet is caused by ego and old code unconscious behaviour? War, violence, wealth theft, corruption, oppression, inequality. These are all old code responses to when egos want more than they need.

As long as you continue trying to satisfy your ego, you will continue acting out old code and continue suffering. Humanity will continue suffering.

To free yourself from ego, to help humanity free itself from collective ego, you must learn to override old code unconscious actions and create new code. Example: If your ego wants you to be resentful, but you choose to be forgiving, you override old code and create new code.

To override old code, you need to practice new code on an action. Override old code with *The 4 Practicable Actions of Love.*

THE 4 PRACTICABLE ACTIONS OF LOVE

Patience (P)
Forgiveness (F)
Gratitude (G)
Compassion (C)

If you want to "practice Love" you need to break down Love into practicable actions.

Love is Oneness. When you feel at one with other people, you have endless patience, forgiveness, gratitude and compassion for yourself and them.

PFGC is how you practice Love.

WHAT IS PATIENCE?

Patience is never giving up on yourself and others.

Shouting, yelling, huffing, puffing, quitting, dismissing, abandoning, rushing, judging, are all forms of losing patience.

Losing patience is the first wall ego builds to separate you from Love. To lose patience with yourself is self-sabotage. To lose patience with others places you in a position of superiority. Both stop progress towards Love.

People think our attention spans are getting shorter. Attention *span* is capacity, how much we have. Our capacity is not decreasing. The ability to *access* our capacity is decreasing. Patience is how you access your full capacity, be it your attention span or your life's potential. We are losing our ability to be patient with ourselves and each other and therefore accessing less of our capacity, less of our potential.

If you think about it, the only thing we have consistent patience for is our own suffering: we do it 30, 50, 80 years without trying something different.

For your own well-being, try something different. Try being patient.

WHAT IS FORGIVENESS?

Forgiveness is letting go of any and all resentments that block *you* from becoming Love.

Ego uses resentments to sustain old code. Example: "My father was cold and never hugged me. Now he's frail and dying and I feel incapable of showing him tenderness." This is how old code blocks Love.

The only way to end the cycle of past old code causing us pain today is to forgive. Forgive your family. Forgive your culture. Forgive another culture. The alternative is to pass on this pain to people not yet born. Is that fair?

We all run on old code. Most people are not purposefully trying to hurt you, they are only slaves to their own old code. You are not purposefully trying to hurt people or yourself, you are only slave to your own old code. Accept that people only do what they are capable of doing at the time. Forgive them like you'd want to be forgiven.

WHAT IS GRATITUDE?

Gratitude is appreciating everything that helps you BECOME LOVE.

You cannot BECOME LOVE in a vacuum. Life is a training ground. Every heartbreak, every disappointment, all the pain in your life has brought you to this moment, the moment you decided to BECOME LOVE. Where would you rather be: stuck repeating old code, or excited to create new code?

We have positive and negative experiences driving us to Love. Positive experiences support your growth, negative experiences push you to change. You need both to BECOME LOVE.

It is important to practice gratitude for positive experiences, otherwise you will become ungrateful. But if you fail to practice gratitude for negative experiences, you will turn them into resentments and fail to BECOME LOVE.

WHAT IS COMPASSION?

Compassion is choosing to care about what another person is feeling.

If you hear someone asking for help, can you stop and offer them your attention? If someone commits a crime, can you try to understand what led them to do it? If someone is in crisis, do you want to offer them support? What does it take to do this? Compassion over judgement.

Losing patience is the first wall ego builds to separate you from Love. Compassion brings down the wall. Forgiveness is letting go of resentments. Compassion is letting go of separateness. Compassion is how you practice Oneness. The feeling of Oneness is joy.

THE 4 PRACTICABLE ACTIONS OF LOVE (PART 2)

PFGC can be broken down further into even more specific practicable actions.

PFGC have 3 QUALITIES:

1. Infinite: Your PFGC never runs out
2. Immediate: There is no delay to your PFGC, it is immediate
3. Unconditional: Your PFGC has no strings attached

PFGC have 2 MODES:

1. Towards yourself
2. Towards others

When you use conscious thoughts and actions to practice patience, forgiveness, gratitude and compassion instead of letting your ego respond with <u>un</u>conscious mentations and actions, you override old code. The more often you override old code the less habitual it becomes. Until finally, PFGC become your new code.

You BECOME LOVE when all of your actions are infinitely, immediately, and unconditionally patient, forgiving, grateful and compassionate towards yourself and others.

This is the greatest gift you can give yourself. To stop your suffering and feel joyful.

This is the greatest gift you can give humanity. Because the more Loving people there are on the planet, the more peaceful the planet becomes.

It's a big, huge task. How do you begin?

Start stand-up meditating.

HOW TO STAND-UP MEDITATE

Stand-up meditating can be difficult until it becomes second-nature. Don't rush through this section.

How can you actually practice Love (PFGC) throughout your day? It's easy to *say*, "Practice infinite patience towards yourself," but how do you actually *do* it? At home? At work? By yourself? In a group?

Conscious Action

Replace old code with new code by putting your PFGC into an action. It can't stay in your head, you must find an action to express it. So if you want to be patient, you must express patience through conscious action. **This is the same as returning your mind to Love during sit-down meditation, only instead of conscious thought, it's conscious action.**

But your mind is untamed. Your ego will mentate, "What is this? I am not patient. Tell this person to hurry up!" This is an unconscious mentation (1). This mentation will give you the urge to say, "Hurry up!" out loud.

This is how unconscious mentation (1) becomes unconscious action (2). This is why you need to sit-down meditate. You sit-down meditate to practice recognizing unconscious mentation *before* it becomes unconscious action. You can't perform unconscious actions while you're sitting with your eyes closed (unless you fidget).

But in the heat of the day, despite your best efforts, unconscious mentation (1) will turn into unconscious action (2). That's okay. You now have an opportunity to practice turning old code into new code. Replace old code with new code by replacing unconscious actions (2) with conscious actions (4). How? Conscious thoughts (3).

The more you practice, the more quickly you will recognize your habitual old code responses as unconscious actions (2). You will see these actions are not Love: impatient, resentful, ungrateful, judgemental. These responses cause you suffering. So pause and think: What action can I take to practice patience, forgiveness, gratitude and compassion instead? This is a conscious thought (3). Then follow-through with the conscious action (4).

This is hard. Overriding old code is hard. You are fighting a lifetime of unconscious behaviour. This is why it's so hard to simply say, "I'm sorry." Conscious actions will feel uncomfortable, perhaps even scary. New code will feel uncomfortable. Don't seek comfort. Seek Love.

Let's say you want to practice immediate forgiveness towards others. You walk in on coworkers gossiping about you. Your ego mentates: "Be hurt. Develop resentment."

This is an unconscious mentation (1). Since you have been practicing sit-down meditation you can recognize the mentation before it becomes unconscious action (2). Instead of perpetuating old code, you can skip unconscious action (2) by using conscious thought (3) to decide, 'I want to practice immediate forgiveness towards others.' So you say to your gossiping coworkers, "Don't worry about it. I'd gossip about me, too." This positive, light-hearted response puts your forgiveness into a conscious action (4).

The more often you practice turning old code into new code, the faster you will become good at it. Eventually, you won't have to stop and reflect that, 'This is unconscious action.' It will become second-nature to replace unconscious mentations and actions with conscious thoughts and actions.

Stand-up meditation is turning unconscious mentations (1) and unconscious actions (2) into conscious thoughts (3) and conscious actions (4) on the fly, throughout your day.

It's just like returning your untamed mind to Love in sit-down meditation, but instead of *thinking* Love, you *do* Love. Do Love always, you *are* Love.

So, what does this look like in everyday life?

The following stories are stand-up meditation practice examples for patience, forgiveness, gratitude and compassion. **The conscious actions (4) are bolded**.

PRACTICE PATIENCE

You must practice patience every day in order to override old code and BECOME LOVE. Practice the 3 QUALITIES of patience: Infinite, Immediate, Unconditional; and the 2 MODES: Towards yourself, Towards others.

INFINITE PATIENCE

Infinite patience is when your patience never runs out.

TOWARDS YOURSELF: You start at a new gym. You feel good the first week, but by the second week you're more tired than ever. You haven't lost weight or gained muscle. Your untamed mind, which doesn't want to be patient, tells you, "I should quit." This is an opportunity to practice infinite patience. You know, logically, if you keep going you will get fitter. It is only your patience that has run out. If you **return to the gym and keep going even when your progress is not noticeable**, you override old code and increase the duration of your patience. Eventually, you will get fitter, and if you keep practicing, you will become more Love.

TOWARDS OTHERS: Your coworker is telling another boring story. Third today. It is your lunchtime. You could be curt and say, "I don't care." If you lose patience with them you are saying your time is more valuable than theirs. Which might be true, but remember, the goal is to BECOME LOVE. Now is the time to practice infinite patience. Instead of being curt, you could **politely say, "I'm sorry, it's my lunch-time, I gotta go."**

IMMEDIATE PATIENCE

Immediate patience is being patient now, instead of looking back later and wishing you were patient. There is no delay in expressing your patience, it is immediate.

TOWARDS YOURSELF: You start reading a book recommended by a friend. It's hard to understand, you can't follow along, you feel dumb, and get frustrated. You want to slam the book down and give up. This is an opportunity to practice immediate patience. **Read one more chapter whether you like it or not. Then decide calmly if you want to give up on the book.** Don't let your frustrated mind's lack of patience dictate your actions.

TOWARDS OTHERS: You are tired; it's been a long day. You are waiting in line at a convenience store. The person in front of you is taking their sweet time buying lottery tickets. Your old code response wants you to say, "Hurry up already!" But the Universe does not revolve around your impatient mind. **Instead, you could wish the person good luck on their selections.** By practicing immediate patience, you are overriding old code with new code. This helps you BECOME LOVE.

UNCONDITIONAL PATIENCE

Unconditional patience is not making any excuses why you can't be patient. Your patience has no strings attached.

TOWARDS YOURSELF: You try to quit something (smoking, biting your nails, eating junk food, spending too much time on social media, so on). Your ego creates the excuse: 'I'll quit when my life slows down (condition), and I can focus.' Now your ego can use old code responses to keep your life moving fast so you never feel ready. Instead, don't let the condition get in the way, **start to quit right now. Have patience it takes time, and recommit after every relapse.** Conditions on yourself are one way your ego self-sabotages your growth. Don't let anything get in the way of you becoming Love.

TOWARDS OTHERS: Your neighbour is being loud. You ask them patiently to lower the noise after a certain time. They get angry. Now you feel justified getting angry too: 'They weren't patient so now I don't have to be.' This is a condition. Practice unconditional patience. **Ask again just as calmly.** Your patience doesn't require their partnership.

*Look for moments to practice patience throughout your day. You can either seek out situations or people that you know will test your patience, or prepare for your patience to be spontaneously challenged.

PRACTICE FORGIVENESS

You must practice forgiveness every day in order to override old code and BECOME LOVE. Practice the 3 QUALITIES of forgiveness: Infinite, Immediate, Unconditional; and the 2 MODES: Towards yourself, Towards others.

INFINITE FORGIVENESS

Infinite forgiveness is when your forgiveness never runs out.

TOWARDS YOURSELF: You blow it with romantic partners. You don't communicate well. You are so fed up with heartbreak you swear off relationships. This is how old code blocks Love today. Instead, the next time someone shows interest, show yourself forgiveness by remaining open and **communicating to them your past mistakes.** This zaps the power of old code by creating new code. Now you are less prone to repeating the mistakes.

TOWARDS OTHERS: A family member repeatedly borrows money and doesn't pay you back. They ask for more money and you deny them. They say awful things to you and cut you out of their life. Understand that by following their old code, they are hurting themselves more than you. Forgiving them doesn't mean lending them more money, you can forgive them by **not talking bad about them at family gatherings**. The practice is about *you* not harbouring Love blocking resentments.

IMMEDIATE FORGIVENESS

Immediate forgiveness is when you can forgive in the moment, rather than holding onto resentment until you're ready to let it go. There is no delay in expressing your forgiveness, it is immediate.

TOWARDS YOURSELF: You yell at someone while driving your car and realize you're expressing road rage. You could beat yourself up the rest of the day, stop all practices, and then forgive yourself tomorrow. Or, you could use the moment to practice immediate forgiveness towards yourself. **Say aloud, "You won that round, ego, but I forgive you for your old code."** The next practice is always in the next situation.

TOWARDS OTHERS: You pass a person on the street panhandling. They appear kind. You tell them you have no money and they instantly turn mean. Your old code will want to lash back. Instead, forgive them for their old code. **Say without hostility, "I'm sorry, next time I'll carry change."** Watch their reaction. Their old code will be starved of oxygen. When you're practicing diligently, this is how fast you can forgive.

UNCONDITIONAL FORGIVENESS

Unconditional forgiveness is not making excuses why you should hold onto resentments. Your forgiveness has no strings attached.

TOWARDS YOURSELF: The person you like likes someone else. You think it's because they are more attractive. You become obsessed with your vanity. A resentment towards yourself forms, 'Until I'm perfect (condition), nobody will like me (insecurity).' To drop this self-inflicted resentment, ask yourself what you'd do if someone you loved told you the same thing. **Give yourself the advice you'd give to them. Listen. Keep listening until you believe.**

TOWARDS OTHERS: You and a friend get into a major fight. You both say hurtful things, but you think they went too far. You could refuse to apologize until they apologize first (condition). Or, **you could pick up the phone and apologize for your part.** That's showing strength, not weakness, because letting go of your resentment usually gives others the strength to let go of theirs.

*Look for moments to practice forgiveness throughout your day. You can either seek out situations or people that you know will test your forgiveness, or prepare for your forgiveness to be spontaneously challenged.

PRACTICE GRATITUDE

You must practice gratitude every day in order to override old code and BECOME LOVE. Practice the 3 QUALITIES of gratitude: Infinite, Immediate, Unconditional; and the 2 MODES: Towards yourself, Towards others.

INFINITE GRATITUDE

Infinite gratitude is when your gratitude never runs out.

TOWARDS YOURSELF: You have less towels than you want. Then you meet someone that doesn't have even one towel. It never even occurred to you someone could not have one towel. Now you feel grateful for having your amount of towels. How can you show gratitude towards yourself for having enough towels? **Give a towel to the person without.** This can apply to towels and to money.

TOWARDS OTHERS: Your ex-spouse continues testing your patience and forgiveness. They are stuck in their old code. You could develop resentments and wage war. Or, you could see them as a sparring partner. They give you opportunities to practice Love. **We thank sparring partners.**

IMMEDIATE GRATITUDE

Immediate gratitude is when you can show appreciation in the moment, rather than in hindsight. There is no delay in expressing your gratitude, it is immediate.

TOWARDS YOURSELF: Three weeks ago you promised to do volunteer work. On the day of volunteering, your friend invites you on a boat ride. Your old code tells you to blow off volunteering. You could submit to old code, or you could override old code and keep your commitment to volunteering, seeing it as an opportunity to practice Love. **Spend 10 more minutes volunteering than you would have to show yourself gratitude for making this new code choice.**

TOWARDS OTHERS: *Positive experience*: A wealthy family member gifts you an item you couldn't otherwise afford. To show gratitude, **say thank you and tell them how you intend to use the item.** *Negative experience*: After thinking about it, a wealthy family member decides not buy you the item you asked for. To show gratitude **say, "Thanks for giving it some thought. I'll wait until I can afford it myself."** It's always your choice to either create an unhelpful resentment (old code), or practice gratitude (new code).

UNCONDITIONAL GRATITUDE

Unconditional gratitude is when you don't invent excuses for why you won't be grateful. Your gratitude has no strings attached.

TOWARDS YOURSELF: You wake up most mornings feeling awful. You go through most days feeling down. You don't know how to stop feeling this way. You are so mad this has become your life. Eventually, you get so fed up with living this way, you vow you will stop at nothing to make a change. You start to practice Love every day, and slowly, you start feeling better. Now you look back at those awful days and regret you ever felt that way. Why? Instead, be grateful for feeling awful, it changed your life. **Treat yourself in some way for sticking to your vow.**

TOWARDS OTHERS: An unrepentant racist runs for office. They win. They govern as a racist. They are so noxious people who never cared about politics now decide to vote in the next election. You run for office opposing the racist. You win. You govern with Love. Now more people are inspired to BECOME LOVE. **Thank the racist for inspiring you in your acceptance speech.**

*Look for moments to practice gratitude throughout your day. You can either seek out situations or people that you know will test your gratitude, or prepare for your gratitude to be spontaneously challenged.

PRACTICE COMPASSION

You must practice compassion every day in order to override old code and BECOME LOVE. Practice the 3 QUALITIES of compassion: Infinite, Immediate, Unconditional; and the 2 MODES: Towards yourself, Towards others.

INFINITE COMPASSION

Infinite compassion is when your compassion never runs out.

TOWARDS YOURSELF: You are months into your Love practice. You have noticeably progressed, others see it, but you still struggle with losing your patience with others. You could become discouraged, judge yourself, and give up. Or you could **give yourself the same advice you'd give someone else progressing towards Love: "Good work. Keep going."**

TOWARDS OTHERS: You have a friend that regularly self-sabotages their life. You help them get a good job. They start off strong then one day rage-quit, making you look bad. How could they put you in this position? Because their old code is still strong. Practice infinite compassion by understanding their timeline to conquer their old code may be longer than your timeline. **Reach out and see what you can do for your friend now.**

IMMEDIATE COMPASSION

Immediate compassion is when you choose compassion over judgement in the moment, rather than in hindsight. There is no delay in expressing your compassion, it is immediate.

TOWARDS YOURSELF: You think you are over old code. Then one day an unexpected challenge brings out an old code resentment. You are able to recognize it, but you can't immediately replace it with new code. You could beat yourself up for not being as far along as you wanted to be. Or, you could immediately choose compassion over judgement by **laughing at yourself and saying, "Good thing I didn't tell everyone I was perfect."** The light-heartedness of this attitude will help you let go of the resentment as well.

TOWARDS OTHERS: You are on the bus. The woman in front of you is constantly checking her appearance on her phone. You could let your old code judge her for being vain. Or, you could feel compassion for a person who feels so insecure about their appearance they need to constantly check. When they get up to leave, **pay them a compliment, or at least acknowledge their presence with a friendly smile.**

UNCONDITIONAL COMPASSION

Unconditional compassion is not creating excuses for why you can't be compassionate. Your compassion has no strings attached.

TOWARDS YOURSELF: You are wealthy but unhappy. You think because you are wealthy that nobody will care about your problems. Your old code judges you, "Keep these problems to yourself, you are too privileged to ask for help." Instead, accept you are human like everyone else, and show yourself compassion by **reaching out for help and support.** This creates new code.

TOWARDS OTHERS: Two countries prepare for war. Your side says the other side hates you, they hate your way of life, they hate your culture. You could jump on the bandwagon and perpetuate this hate; this creates endless hate. Or, you could **reach out to the other country's ethnic community near you and start a dialogue. Say, "I don't hate you, I Love you. How can we stop this fighting?"** You may not avert the war, but you won't be made into an unwilling soldier.

*Look for moments to practice compassion throughout your day. You can either seek out situations or people that you know will test your compassion, or prepare for your compassion to be spontaneously challenged.

When you can be infinitely, immediately and unconditionally patient, forgiving, grateful and compassionate towards yourself and others, you have BECOME LOVE.

Humanity desperately needs more Loving people. Right this second.

STAND-UP MEDITATION: REVIEW

What do all these practices add up to?

The 4 Practicable Actions of Love x 3 QUALITIES x 2 MODES = 24 specific practices to override old code, create new code, practice and BECOME LOVE.

Ask yourself in every situation throughout your day: "How can I practice Love (PFGC) right now?" Then choose a practice (example: unconditional gratitude towards yourself) and stand-up meditate by putting your practice into an action.

You will not be able to stand-up meditate without sit-down meditation. Your mind is untamed, it doesn't listen to you. Sit-down meditation will train you to recognize <u>un</u>conscious mentations and actions so you are able to replace them with conscious thoughts and actions, in the moment. This is why you need sit-down meditation. Becoming Love starts with butt down and eyes closed.

Then you can stand-up meditate, turning any situation into an opportunity to practice Love: You can be patient when yelled at. You can be forgiving when heartbroken. You can be grateful when nothing goes right. You can be compassionate when the world goes mad around you.

Countless times your instinct will be to revert to old code. That is countless opportunities to replace old code with new code. Every time you do, you are stand-up meditating.

Sit-down meditate so you are able to stand-up meditate.

Stand-up meditate to override old code and create new code by practicing patience, forgiveness, gratitude and compassion through conscious action, throughout your day.

This is how you BECOME LOVE.

Now it's time to go all in.

STEP 3: FULL-TIME MEDITATION

YOUR NUMBER ONE GOAL

You have to want to BECOME LOVE more than anything you have ever wanted. More than all your egoic fantasies combined. More than your most greedy, lusty, wildest ambitions. To BECOME LOVE—so you can stop suffering, feel joyful and help humanity live in peace—needs to be your number one goal. Only with that level of resolve will you overcome your deepest, most unconscious old code.

It will take time to wrestle your mind from the old ways of old code to the new ways of new code. Then one day it will click: What your ego wants no longer matters. Becoming Love is all that matters. That change in perspective will come with time.

For a while you are going to think practicing Love is something separate from the rest of your life. As you deepen your practice you will realize it's all intertwined: What you eat, how you treat your family, how you interact with other people, what you do for a living, *is* your Love practice. Weave Love into your daily life and responsibilities.

The more fully you can integrate every area of your life towards this goal, cutting out anything that holds you back, the faster you will progress.

When you use every situation throughout your day to practice Love, you make your life a full-time meditation.

Whenever you're ready:

WORK BACKWARDS

Work backwards by imagining you have already BECOME LOVE—paint a picture in your mind.

What do you look like? What do you sound like? Then go deeper. What do you eat? What time do you eat? What do you wear? Where can you practice? Who do you practice with? How does Love influence what you do for a living?

Take a few minutes and capture that picture in your mind. Imagine you are Love right down to the minute details. Once you have identified those details, they are your road-map to becoming Love.

Follow your road-map; do not become distracted by things not on your road. This is discipline. Discipline is the foundation to achieving goals.

Commit to following your road-map in stages.

COMMIT IN STAGES

BECOME LOVE: The new goal for your life. It's a full-life goal. **Either you practice Love or you perpetuate old code**. Eventually, you must stop everything that blocks Love. But change takes time.

Commit to becoming Love in stages. Don't let ego throw up a road-block, "I can't commit 100% right now, let's wait until I can." Nonsense.

Start by sit-down meditating. Make that a habit. Then stand-up meditate once or twice a day. Go out and look for situations to practice patience. Make that a habit. Then add forgiveness. Then gratitude. Then compassion. Look for situations to practice with yourself. Then with your family. Then with your friends. Then with your colleagues.

And start noticing when you self-sabotage your progress.

STOP SELF-SABOTAGE

Self-sabotage is any behaviour that prevents you from practicing Love, and/or practices unconscious behaviour.

Self-sabotage is how ego sustains old code. Your ego is not interested in ceding control of your untamed mind. All ego knows is old code, even if that causes you suffering. Ego will do anything to stop you replacing old code with new.

Example: You start making PFGC progress. You feel good. You decide to celebrate by partying. You wake up tired and forget to practice PFGC. This is how ego self-sabotages.

It's important to remember: Your ego is not a villain plotting your demise. Ego is just an extremely old unconscious desire to be separate inherited down the generations. Don't hate your ego. Practice PFGC even for your ego.

Reflect on how you 'celebrate,' 'relax,' or 'unwind'—are you acting consciously during these times? If you're not, then you're practicing unconscious thoughts and actions. This makes it harder to practice conscious thoughts and actions when you want to.

Which doesn't mean practicing Love is no fun. What you find fun will change the more Loving you become. Enjoy the transition. Practice PFGC even for your self-sabotage.

Watch out for common forms of self-sabotage: excessive partying; excessive entertainment; feeling pessimistic about your ability to change; purposefully creating and perpetuating drama in your life; adopting popular societal beliefs about money and status to fit-in; pushing people away that are trying to help you; thinking you are already perfect and it's everyone else that needs to change.

Use stand-up meditation conscious actions to replace old code self-sabotage with new code healthy behaviour.

STAND-UP MEDITATION FOR SELF-SABOTAGE

Example: Endlessly scrolling social media with no purpose is self-sabotage. You are avoiding the unconscious mentations you need to become aware of, because only then can you replace them with conscious thoughts. Use conscious action to replace scrolling with practicing Love. Ego will mentate, 'Too much work, I'd rather zone-out.' This is unconscious mentation. Stop the unconscious action of scrolling by using conscious thought to remember, 'I need to stop self-sabotaging in order to stop suffering and feel joyful.' Use conscious action to put down the phone and practice sit-down meditation, whether your untamed mind wants to or not. When your 15 minutes of sit-down meditation are over, don't go back to the phone, find someone to talk to. Sincerely ask how they are doing, listen, and respond with PFGC.

Stopping self-sabotage is not easy, but every time you replace old code with new code, the power your ego has over you diminishes. Conversely, every time you self-sabotage, you give your ego more power.

Don't power your ego with ego entertainment.

WHAT IS EGO ENTERTAINMENT?

Entertainment about people acting out unconsciously, motivated by their egos. Basically, people being bad to one another without ever trying to change their behaviour. Your ego likes ego entertainment. Your ego likes watching people abusing, hurting, stealing from and controlling other people, because this is how ego survives in our minds and in our world. You can practice PFGC all-day, but you'll make little progress if you entertain your ego all-night.

Most people use ego entertainment to self-medicate. Living an ego-driven life is such suffering you want to turn on the TV and 'escape'. But there is no 'escape' from life, there is only taking a break from dealing with your unconscious mentations. Every time you 'escape' from your unconscious mentations, you give them more power, you give your ego more power. Giving ego more power sustains your suffering.

The more you let your ego fantasize, the less you let your Love realize. Ego entertainment is self-sabotage.

Or, you can be entertained by people trying their best to practice Love. This is conscious entertainment. Conscious entertainment is rare, but it's a valuable tool in the goal to BECOME LOVE. When you can find it, support it. When you can't find it, demand it. And if you can make it, make it.

NO EXCUSES

Excuses are self-sabotage. The most popular excuses to get out of having to practice Love are, "I'm too dumb," "I'm not smart enough," "I'm not good enough," "People can't change." Don't believe it, your self-sabotaging ego is playing games with you.

Tell your ego, "Enough is enough, it's time for me to BECOME LOVE. If I practice every day I will be free from you and feel joyful. I will change."

Your ego will keep making excuses and it's up to you to decide who is in charge of your life.

Nobody is too dumb to meditate, sit-down or stand-up; there is nobody not smart enough to BECOME LOVE. Your ego is lying to you. Everyone can change. You *can* become the most patient, forgiving, grateful, compassionate and Loving version of yourself. To do this, you have to learn to believe in yourself. You're ready. It's time to stop making excuses.

It's better to just have a short memory.

SHORT MEMORY

You will suck. You will attempt to practice immediate forgiveness and your ego will laugh and stay resentful. You will feel like a failure. You are not, you just need more sit-down meditation.

You will practice unconditional compassion and the other person's ego will shut you down, make you feel embarrassed for even trying. Develop a short memory.

You practiced; it's all you can do. Move on to the next situation. Eventually your Love becomes so strong it's undeniable. Until then practice and move on.

Don't let a world full of threatened egos stop you from becoming Love.

BILLIONS OF EGOS

You think battling with one ego is a challenge? Try battling with billions.

No ego likes losing control. Not yours, not someone else's. Prepare to be challenged. Out-of-control egos will seek you out. Take it as a compliment. You have been labelled a threat. A threat to ego is a hero to humanity.

Just remember the hero is not you. **The hero is Love**. You are becoming Love. When it becomes about you becoming the hero, that's ego creating a blind spot.

EGO BLIND SPOT

So you start to practice Love every day. You feel the results. People are drawn to you. People want to help you. People ask your advice.

Do you feel powerful? Ego loves power. Your ego will want to make becoming Love a selfish goal, a goal to become super, powerful. This is how ego creates a massive blind spot to sneak back up on you. This is how good leaders become corrupt leaders.

Becoming Love is not about you gaining power, it's about spreading the power of Love. All you have to do is seek situations to practice Love and let Love do the work. To do this, seek situations that will challenge your PFGC rather than situations that make you feel comfortable.

This will be scary at first.

Use this guide to help you.

USE THIS GUIDE

This guide is written as a reminder. All you have to do is read the guide and you will be placed back into the correct headspace needed to BECOME LOVE.

If you can only practice Love for a few hours or a few days at a time before forgetting and regressing to your old way of life, then you need to read this guide every day. Not the entire guide, just the sections you are struggling with. Use this guide.

Don't worry if you have to return to the guide often, this is a new way of life, it will take time to become a habit.

If you've stopped practicing and you don't know how to restart, this is how to reset.

HOW TO RESET

Life will get in the way. You will forget to practice Love. You will forget to even want to practice. You are stuck in unconscious mentations (1) and unconscious actions (2). Maybe you had a bad night's sleep. Maybe you're fighting with your partner. Work is too busy. Whatever. You have lost track that your goal in life is to BECOME LOVE.

This is how to reset:

STOP self-sabotaging
(endlessly scrolling social media; being argumentative; excessive partying);

SLEEP: take a nap
(no alarm, wake-up naturally);

SIT-down meditate
(minimum one cycle of repeating the words, working back up to five cycles);

STAND-up meditate
(deliberately seek PFGC practice situations)

Repeat this process every day, whether your untamed mind wants to or not, until you are back on track.

Join a Become Love Group to help keep you on track.

BECOME LOVE GROUPS

You will find it helpful to meet with others who have set out to BECOME LOVE. You can share experiences, get feedback and support each other's practices.

These don't have to be formal meetings, four to eight friends getting together once a week at someone's house counts as a Group. Even as few as two people sitting at a coffee shop counts as a Group.

It's harder to learn without feedback, and the Groups are a way to get regular feedback from compassionate people who also understand the challenge of becoming Love. But try not to make the Groups into advice sessions. You are not trying to 'fix' each other. You are there to support. If advice is solicited, give it. If not, just listen. Listening is compassionate.

Take turns discussing any breakthroughs or challenges you are having with your sit-down and stand-up meditation practices throughout the week. If comfortable, share some of your self-sabotage challenges. If possible, end every Group with 15 minutes of sit-down meditation.

You can set weekly goals for the Group, like: Everyone sit-down meditates twice a day. Or, everyone practices immediate patience once a day. Be kind if not everyone reaches the goal. This is a great place to practice unconditional compassion towards others.

Attending a Become Love Group regularly will help keep you focused on the goal, which can be difficult in our busy lives.

To help yourself stay focused between Groups, repeat the goal.

REPEAT LOVE

Between sit-down and stand-up meditation practices, repeat the goal to yourself silently: "Love."

While you're walking to work, say to yourself silently: "Love... Love... Love..."

While you're waiting in line...

While watching your dog run at the park...

While falling asleep....

"Love... Love... Love... Love... Love... Love..."

***Avoid repetition of the goal when you should be concentrating on something possibly dangerous: driving, using tools, etc. Repeat when appropriate.**

You can start taking walks while repeating 'Love'. Use these walks as healthy breaks.

Challenge yourself to repeat Love for a defined period of time. Instead of scrolling on your phone while waiting for an appointment, repeat Love until you're called. Or, when you're riding an escalator or elevator, repeat Love until you have to get off.

Repeat Love instead of drowning out life with headphones. This is sending out a message to the world that you do not want connection. This is practicing separateness. There are times for that, but it's unhelpful to practice it frequently. Instead, practice Oneness by repeating Love.

Between sit-down and stand-up meditation, *The 4 Practicable Actions of Love* and repeating Love, your mind will always be on Love. When your mind and thoughts are always on Love, your actions will BECOME LOVE. When all of your actions are Love, you *are* Love.

When you are Love, you stop suffering.

When enough of us are Love, we stop hurting each other.

When humanity becomes Love, we live in peace.

This is the goal.

Track your progress towards the goal with a Log.

BECOME LOVE LOG

Keep a Log of your daily efforts towards becoming Love. Keep the entries simple. This Log is not a place for your ego to comment on your practices, or to beat yourself up in text. This Log is simply about keeping track of what happened.

First, write the date at the top, then divide the page into sections for:

- SIT-DOWN MEDITATION
- REPEAT LOVE
- STAND-UP MEDITATION (PFGC)
- SELF-SABOTAGE
- BECOME LOVE GROUP

You want to document your successes, but you don't want to judge yourself for failures. Simply acknowledge what happened.

For instance, in the SIT-DOWN MEDITATION section, write when you sat and for how many cycles. That's it. If you didn't sit-down meditate that day, simply write:

"Didn't sit-down meditate today, didn't want to, couldn't motivate myself."

You do <u>not</u> need to add judgement:

"Didn't sit-down meditate today, I feel guilty, I'll never be good at this, what's wrong with me?"

Same goes for the STAND-UP MEDITATION section where you log your patience, forgiveness, gratitude and compassion practices for that day. Document when you were able to override old code with a (+) symbol, and simply acknowledge when you couldn't with a (-) symbol. For example:

"P-: Lost patience with a coworker, patience ran out, not infinite, couldn't override old code."

You do <u>not</u> need to make judgements on what happened:

"P-: Lost patience with a coworker, I'm so stupid, I should know better."

*See more examples of simply starting what happened in the EXAMPLE LOG below.

For the REPEAT LOVE section, write down any times you repeated 'Love' to yourself for more than a few seconds. If you didn't repeat Love at all that day, write that. Try again tomorrow.

For SELF-SABOTAGE, log anything you did that prevented you from practicing Love that day, as well as any times you practiced <u>un</u>conscious behaviour. So if you could have satdown meditated, but you were too tired because you were up late playing video games, then log that. Or if you decided to scroll social media instead of stand-up meditating, log that. If you got into a needless argument with someone and you don't even know why, that was probably self-sabotage.

You will have to be hard on yourself without judging yourself in this section. Be honest when you self-sabotaged, but don't fixate on it. Just log it. Use the Log to avoid this behaviour in the future. If you were able to stop self-sabotaging behaviour, or replace it with new code healthy behaviour, log that too.

Finally, in the BECOME LOVE GROUP section, note whether you attended a group that day, either in-person or online. If you didn't, just write that.

Re-read your Log every day. As the Log grows, you will start to see where you have improved, and where you can still improve, so you can put focus on those areas. For instance, if you notice you consistently hold onto resentments, make practicing immediate forgiveness a focus for the next day. If you notice you consistently self-sabotage as soon as you get home from work, prepare something healthy to do instead. Or sit-down meditate.

It doesn't matter what form the Log takes: handwritten, typewritten, on computer or phone—whatever you feel most comfortable keeping handy.

EXAMPLE BECOME LOVE LOG

JANUARY 1, 20XX

SIT-DOWN MEDITATION

+ Sat-down meditated after waking up, 5 cycles

or...

- Didn't sit today, didn't want to, couldn't motivate myself

REPEAT LOVE

+ On the way to the gym
+ While waiting in line for coffee

or...

- Didn't remember today

STAND-UP MEDITATION (PFGC)

P-: Lost patience with a coworker, patience ran out, not infinite, couldn't override old code.

F+: Immediately forgave slow fast food server, smiled and said thank you, created new code.

G-: Didn't tell mom I was grateful for dinner, forgot, wasn't aware enough to remember.

C+: Showed compassion for stranger that looked lost, helped them with directions, went out of my way to do this, created new code.

SELF-SABOTAGE

- Stayed up late last night playing video games, made me too tired to sit-down in the morning

- Could have sat-down before lunch, but scrolled social media instead

- Ate more junk food after work than I planned

- Got into an argument with friend, was too upset to practice for rest of the day

+ Went for a walk instead of buying cigarettes

BECOME LOVE GROUP

+ Attended in-person
or....
- Didn't go

FULL-TIME MEDITATION: REVIEW

BECOME LOVE: a better goal for your life.

All of your actions are infinitely, immediately, and unconditionally patient, forgiving, grateful and compassionate towards yourself and others.

The only way to stop suffering, feel joyful and help humanity live in peace.

To do this, learn to override unconscious thoughts and actions (old code, ego) with conscious thoughts and actions (new code, Love). This is called **TAMING YOUR MIND**.

STEP 1: SIT-DOWN MEDITATION is how you replace unconscious thoughts with conscious thoughts.

STEP 2: STAND-UP MEDITATION is how you replace unconscious thoughts and actions with conscious thoughts and actions throughout your day by practicing patience, forgiveness, gratitude and compassion (PFGC).

STEP 3: FULL-TIME MEDITATION, use every situation throughout your day to practice Love.

STOP SELF-SABOTAGE, any behaviour that blocks you from practicing Love, and/or practices unconscious behaviour.

Join a **BECOME LOVE GROUP** to get feedback and support from others.

REPEAT LOVE to keep your mind focused on the goal.

Keep a **BECOME LOVE LOG** of your daily efforts towards becoming Love.

And one final, final reminder: What we mean when we say, "This world needs more Love," is really, "This world needs more Loving people." **You BECOME LOVE by practicing Love**. So practice. That's a huge contribution.

Good Love,

ALEXANDER DE JORDY has been obsessed for almost a decade with developing a practical way to BECOME LOVE so we can all finally live in peace. He lives in Toronto, where he's going back to school to become a paramedic.

You can hire Alexander as a Become Love Coach.
For more information, email:

alexander@becomelove.ca

The Coaching Edition of this guide will be released Fall, 2024.

A Become Love Log available for purchase, and a Become Love App, are in the works.

If you would like to give feedback on *The Guide*, please visit:

www.becomelove.ca/feedback

Made in the USA
Las Vegas, NV
19 February 2024

85972092R00052